W9-BML-327

The Journey Ahead

· Believing in Ourselves ·

The Journey Ahead

A Book for Women

Arlene F. Benedict

Ariel Books

·

**Andrews McMeel
Publishing**

Kansas City

www.andrewsmcmeel.com

ISBN: 0-8362-2655-0

Contents

Introduction

What is our destiny? How do we seek it, find it, create it, sustain it? How can we know which path is right for us and recognize it when it appears? Who are the proper role models for us—women who have lived lives rich in purpose and joyful in dedication to their destiny? This book will guide you through an exploration of these questions. As you read and contemplate each essay, you will become more confident about setting out on your journey and enjoying the process.

> You are what your deep, driving desire is.
> As your desire is, so is your will.
> As your will is, so is your deed.
> As your deed is, so is your destiny.
>
> —Brihadaranyaka Upanishad 4:4–5

What Is Our Journey?

Our journey . . . is a tapestry that we weave

Have you ever gazed in awe at a beautiful tapestry? Have you marveled at a Navajo rug, whose designs are woven with such vision and skill? These works of art carry profound lessons for us in our role as life-weavers.

When a weaver begins her work, she creates a design in her mind, but often does not commit herself to a final pattern. As she works, she steps back from her loom frequently to see how it is progressing. If the design isn't coming out the way she envisioned, she pulls out the yarn and begins again. If the pattern is too busy, she simplifies it. If the design needs depth, she adds a new color or texture. Always she keeps in mind the feeling she wants to convey in the final product.

As weavers of our own lives, we, too, must create a mental picture of our destiny—our vision of who we want to become and what we want to accomplish. To make that vision come true, we must become as proud as a weaver. It is up to us to select the patterns and colors of our lives. It is up to us to step back from our lives frequently, to judge how pleased we are and decide what changes we want to make. It is up to us to take great care with the life we are weaving and create a design of beauty and balance.

Today, I will weave my life with care and pride, taking time to step back and look at what I am creating.

The final forming of a person's character lies in their own hands.

—Anne Frank

·

Nothing contributes so much to tranquilize the mind
as a steady purpose—a point on which the soul
may fix its intellectual eye.

—Mary Wollstonecraft Shelley

·

The strongest principle of growth lies in human choice.

—George Eliot

Stars have too long been symbols of the unattainable. They should not be so. For although our physical hands cannot reach them, we can touch them in other ways. Let stars stand for those things which are ideal and radiant in life; if we seek sincerely and strive hard enough, it is possible to reach them, even though the goals seem distant at the onset. And how often do we touch stars when we find them close by in the shining lives of great souls, in the sparkling universe of humanity around us!

—Esther Baldwin York

Find the passion. It takes great passion and great energy to do anything creative. I would go so far as to say you can't do it without that passion.

—Agnes DeMille

*Our journey . . . is our vision of who we are and
what we contribute to the world*

Every great life begins with a dream and every great dream is built around a picture or vision. Anything we can envision clearly, we can make happen.

In our own way, we are like the Olympic gymnast who visualizes her routine. She closes her eyes and sees herself executing the leaps and turns. She feels her body move. She pictures her poise and balance and her final, perfect landing. And if she is able to see it clearly, then she is able to do it physically.

This kind of visualization belongs in our own daily routines. Like a dedicated athlete, we should take time out each day to create some silence and focus on our goals and movements. We owe it to ourselves to make a special time, and perhaps a special place, for reflection. There, we can sit in silence, breathe slowly, and let go of the tensions and turbulence of everyday life.

In the rhythm of our own heartbeats and the quiet of our own breath will come the confidence and clarity of vision we need. Then we can visualize the people we want to help, or the goals we want to reach. Then we can see ourselves doing and becoming that which we dream.

Today, I will envision myself doing the things I dream of doing and being the person I long to be.

The first duty of a human being is to find your real job and do it.
—Charlotte Perkins Gilman

•

No woman should be shamefaced in attempting, through
her work, to give back to the world a portion of its lost heart.
—Louise Bogan

•

Reach high, for stars lie hidden in your soul.
Dream deep, for every dream precedes the goal.
—Pamela Starr

Once you know who you are, you don't have to worry any more.
—Nikki Giovanni

•

Our feelings are our most genuine paths to knowledge.
They are chaotic, sometimes painful, sometimes contradictory,
but they come from deep within us. And we must key into
those feelings. . . . This is how new visions begin.
—Audre Lorde

We don't see things as they are, we see them as we are.

—Anaïs Nin

•

Some of the most important things in life aren't things.

—Linda Ellerbee

•

We need visions for larger things, for the unfolding
and reviewing of worthwhile things.

—Mary McLeod Bethune

Our journey . . . is something we choose—
not a fate that is predetermined for us

Our destiny is not prearranged. Our fate is not written somewhere, waiting for us to follow the script. We create our own fate by the choices we make and the decisions we follow every day.

Often we need courage to break out of a pattern that our friends and family members have followed and expect us to follow as well. Sometimes we have to stand up to people—including, perhaps, our parents—who believe they know what will come. Always we must summon our deepest creativity and will to see ourselves differently from the way others see us, to reject the easy method, to try the untried path.

Creating our own destiny means not accepting the popular or predefined life. It means authoring our particular lives and claiming the right and responsibility to shape our future for ourselves.

Of course, it would be foolish to ignore all advice and invent everything from scratch. We have many friends and relatives who will share the lessons of their own lives if we ask them. We can welcome their insights, respect their views, and be thankful for what they share with us. Then we must proceed to glean what is applicable to us and let the rest go. This may require that we stand firm in our beliefs and vision and resist being swayed by their certainty.

With respect for them and loyalty to ourselves, we listen, consider, decide, set our course, and move on.

Today, I will create my own destiny, by choosing what I know is right for me.

Imagination is the highest kite you can fly.

—Lauren Bacall

•

Pain nourishes courage. You can't be brave if
you've only had wonderful things happen to you.

—Mary Tyler Moore

•

I am old enough to know that victory is often a thing deferred,
and rarely at the summit of courage. . . . What is at the summit
of courage, I think, is freedom. The freedom that comes with
the knowledge that no earthly thing can break you.

—Paula Giddings

Of course I realized there was a measure of danger.
Obviously I faced the possibility of not returning
when first I considered going. Once faced and settled
there really wasn't any good reason to refer to it.

—Amelia Earhart

•

Anticipate the good so that you may enjoy it.

—Ethiopian proverb

•

When people keep telling you that you
can't do a thing, you kind of like to try it.

—Margaret Chase Smith

Our journey . . . is a path we create for ourselves one step at a time

Our destiny is not an end point, like a Fourth of July fireworks finale or a big, ripe apple waiting to be picked. It is a path that forks in two or branches out in several directions before us, and it is up to us to follow the path we consider best. We create our destiny each time we make a decision or choose one path over another.

We make our choices instinctively most of the time, although on occasion we do take time to plan, to lay out steps and contemplate their likely consequences. This is good unless we let planning take the place of action.

Action alone causes movement and progress. It is only in action that we can test ourselves, receive feedback from our world and the people in it, and make rapid course corrections. It is through action that we declare who we are and take a stand for what we hold dear.

In order for our actions to create the desired result, we should set standards by which we make our choices. If we test our decisions against our beliefs and values, then we will always be making progress in the right direction. Sometimes our choices will turn out to be mistakes; occasionally we will head off on a tangent. But we can always get back on track if we know the direction we seek.

Today, I will take action to create my destiny. With each step I will ask: "Does this choice take me in the right direction?" Above all, I will act.

The only adults I know who are marching along their
one true course are boring, insensitive, or lucky.

—Ellen Goodman

•

My favorite thing is to go where I've never been.

—Diane Arbus

•

To follow, without halt, one aim:
There's the secret of success.

—Anna Pavlova

Far away there in the sunshine are my highest aspirations.
I may not reach them but I can look up and see their beauty,
believe in them, and try to follow where they lead.

—Louisa May Alcott

•

I believe the second half of one's life is meant to be better
than the first half. The first half is finding out how you do it.
And the second half is enjoying it.

—Frances Lear

•

I might have been born in a hovel, but I was determined
to travel with the wind and the stars.

—Jacqueline Cochran

*O*ne woman's journey: Barbara Jordan, lawmaker

As a young girl in Texas, Barbara Jordan always told herself she would become something unusual: "I never wanted to be run-of-the-mill." Yet, she never knew what her goal would be. She simply did her best in school, prayed, and waited for the inspiration to come. And so it did, in the person of a black woman lawyer who spoke at Barbara's high school on career day.

From that day on, Barbara was certain of her path and let nothing get in her way—not segregated buses in Houston, not the loneliness of moving to Boston for law school, not the bias she encountered as she began practicing law, not the daunting challenge of representing Texas in the United States Congress. Always she looked for ways to help the greatest number of people to enjoy fully their birthright of liberty.

Barbara made each decision in her life with great joy. Anyone who heard her make a speech, whether to a presidential nominating convention or a congressional committee, knew immediately that this woman of passion truly loved her work. Lawmaking is serious business; Barbara did it with delight and unflagging energy, as if the long hours and heated debates only made her stronger.

She can be an inspiration to all of us who long to make a difference in the world but do not know where to start. Sometimes, just being our best creates the opening we need. Once we see the direction we must take, courage will keep us on our path, joy and passion will be our source of staying power.

Today, I will be my best in whatever I do and stay alert for the voice of destiny as it calls to me.

The days you work are the best days.

—Georgia O'Keeffe

•

It's amazing how fast doors open to us
when we dare to take control of a situation.

—Catherine Ponder

People don't pay much attention to you when you
are second-best. I wanted to see what it felt
like to be number one.

—Florence Griffith-Joyner

It is the soul's duty to be loyal to its own desires.
It must abandon itself to its master passion.

—Rebecca West

You will do foolish things, but do them with enthusiasm.

—Colette

•

Success breeds confidence.

—Beryl Markham

On Our Journey

On our journey . . . we must seek inspiration and guidance

We are travelers through life, always making choices of direction and horizon. Some paths are less traveled than others, yet we are not the first to take them. There is always someone who can guide us at every stage of our journey.

Sometimes our best guide will be a mentor or champion, who will intercede for us, coach us, share lessons from his or her life. This intervention will not prevent us from learning or make it easy for us, but will help us to step truer and faster than we might otherwise be able to do.

Sometimes our best guide will be a writer, minister, or counselor, whose insight into human nature may provide a key we seek. These guides can help us understand our own motives and pull forth our deepest fortitude and creativity. From them, we seek encouragement and support.

At other times we may need help from sources of spiritual strength and wisdom. Whether we go to church, walk in the forest, or meditate by the sea, we owe it to ourselves to develop a rich spiritual life, to sustain us as we travel.

But what about self-reliance? It is necessary, of course, but beware: Going it alone may not be a sign of courage, but of stubborn pride. Yes, we must be captains of our own destinies, but we should not overlook the value of a good navigator from time to time.

Today, I will seek advice and insight, weigh the counsel I receive, and then make my decision with greater certainty.

The formula for success is simple:
Do your best and someone might like it.

—Marva Collins

·

There are few human beings who receive the truth,
complete and staggering, by instant illumination.
Most of them acquire it fragment by fragment,
on a small scale, by successive developments, all
wearily, like a laborious mosaic.

—Anaïs Nin

It is impossible to withhold education from the receptive mind,
as it is impossible to force it upon the unreasoning.

—Agnes Repplier

•

It's better to be a lion for a day than a sheep all your life.

—Sister Elizabeth Kenny

On our journey . . . we must believe in ourselves

The one person we must always be able to count on for praise and encouragement is the one we see in the mirror each morning. Too often, however, we are critical of ourselves, or question our ability to reach our goals or overcome obstacles. We mutter and doubt and discourage our own projects and then we wonder why we long for a supportive voice!

If we cannot say good things about ourselves, who will? If we cannot turn to ourselves for comfort, to whom can we turn? We must be our own best cheerleaders. We must look for and honor what is good and brave and creative about ourselves. When we set a high goal or select a difficult path, we must believe that we will succeed, in spite of all difficulties.

We should not be afraid to paint ourselves larger than life in our dreams and plans. Think of ourselves as heroines and winners and so we shall become! Listen not to those who question our ability to reach our goals. Take advice, yes; take on the anchors of limitation or doubt, no. Trust your own judgment and have faith in your instincts.

Whatever we choose, we should do it with confidence. We must encourage ourselves in the journey and delight in every step of the way. With our self-esteem to back us, we will be proud of our progress and unafraid of the challenges to come.

Today, I will trust and encourage myself and believe that whatever I dream I can accomplish.

We must not, in trying to think about how we can make a big difference, ignore the small daily differences we can make which, over time, add up to big differences that we often cannot foresee.

—Marian Wright Edelman

•

When I'm pushing myself, testing myself,
that's when I'm happiest.
That's when the rewards are greatest.

—Sissy Spacek

Never compromise yourself.
You are all you've got.

—Betty Ford

•

There does not have to be powerlessness.
The power is within ourselves.

—Faye Wattleton

Once I decide to do something,
I can't have people telling me I can't.
If there's a roadblock, you jump over it,
walk around it, crawl under it.

—Kitty Kelley

•

The future belongs to those who believe
in the beauty of their dreams.

—Eleanor Roosevelt

*O*n our journey . . . we must seize the day

Today is a precious gift that will disappear with the night. It should be used to its fullest measure. When we seek our destiny or pursue a goal, every hour can make the difference between going forward and standing still. Every hour can offer the chance to learn something priceless or meet someone wonderful. We must savor each hour and fill each day.

A day is a treasure to be invested, not spent. Why waste it in meaningless pastimes or idle gossip? Why cheat ourselves of even one moment to grow in the direction we seek? How much better it is to dedicate each day to learning and love and growth and health and spiritual peace. How much wiser we are to seize any chance to fulfill our dreams, making every day of our lives count.

This does not mean that we can never rest. Rest itself is an important part of each day: the time to replenish our physical and mental and spiritual balance. But resting need not mean losing momentum.

To seize the day means to step up to every challenge as it presents itself. To seize the day means to greet each morning with vigor and eagerness, no matter what the weather or agenda. To seize the day means to take every chance to progress on our journey of self-discovery and fulfillment.

Today, I will invest my time in progress, growth, and joy.

It's never too late to be what you might have been.

—George Eliot

•

Begin doing what you want to do now.
We are not living in eternity.
We have only this moment,
sparkling like a star in our hand—
and melting like a snowflake.

—Marie Beynon Ray

We don't have an eternity to realize our
dreams, only the time we are here.

—Susan King Taylor

•

I don't want to get to the end of my life
and find that I just lived the length of it.
I want to have lived the width of it as well.

—Diane Ackerman

As I grow older, part of my emotional survival
plan must be to actively seek inspiration instead of
passively waiting for it to find me.

—Bebe Moore Campbell

•

Life is too short to short yourself on life.

—Terri Zadra

On our journey . . . we must dare the impossible

In a quest to find and fulfill our destiny, we must encourage ourselves to dream beyond the limits of what seems realistic or achievable. To curb our vision within the boundaries of what is imaginable would prevent us from doing or becoming that which is, to most people, beyond their wildest dreams.

And boundaries such as these will never propel us to greatness. We must teach ourselves to operate without limitations imposed by the understanding or experience of those around us. We must encourage ourselves to dare what we can scarcely dream of daring. If we do not attempt the impossible, we cannot attain it.

Boldness must be our constant companion. Fearless inventiveness must be the engine that propels us. We must always seek our heart's desire and not shrink our dreams to fit the frames of reference that surround us. We must summon the courage to speak up for what we dream or believe. We should take a leap of faith into the unknown regions.

Yet boldness, on occasion, may require small steps (to build and maintain momentum), rather than large ones. It makes no difference, as long as we are moving forward. Always must we look ahead and up, never back or down.

Above all, we must never abandon our dreams. We must hold them in our minds, plan for them, visualize their happening, prepare for them, move toward them, expect them, watch for them, and talk about them as a reality. And they cannot help coming true.

Today, I will dare the impossible and believe that it will come true.

To struggle and battle and overcome and
absolutely defeat every force designed against
us is the only way to achieve.

—Nannie Burroughs

•

You may have to fight a battle more than once to win it.

—Margaret Thatcher

One isn't necessarily born with courage, but
one is born with potential. Without courage, we cannot
practice any other virtue with consistency. We can't
be kind, true, merciful, generous, or honest.

—Maya Angelou

•

I used to want the words
"She tried" on my tombstone.
Now I want "She did it."

—Katherine Dunham

It is not easy to be a pioneer—but oh, it is fascinating!
I would not trade one moment, even the worst moment,
for all the riches in the world.

—Elizabeth Blackwell

•

Life is either always a tightrope or a feather bed.
Give me the tightrope.

—Edith Wharton

•

If it's a good idea, go ahead and do it.
It is much easier to apologize than
it is to get permission.

—Admiral Grace Murray Hopper

*On our journey . . . we must learn
from mistakes and move on*

Whenever we take on a new challenge, we should expect to stumble from time to time. When that happens, we must decide what that misstep will mean to us.

A stumble, after all, is just a stumble—it has no inherent meaning except the meaning we give to it. We can choose to see it as a sign that we are unsuited to the challenge. We can choose to be demoralized or to turn back from our goal. Or we can choose to use it as an opportunity to learn.

After all, when we were nine months old, a stumble was good news. It meant that we were trying new, brave things, like standing or walking. Why, now that we are older, should a stumble mean anything else? It is simply a reminder to slow down for a brief moment, to look around, to learn what caused the fall, to figure out how to overcome the obstacle or improve our skills in the future. Then, just as we did as babies, we should simply get up and start walking forward again.

When we fall down or lose our way, when we meet with delay or frustration, we should give ourselves the benefit of the doubt. This stumble is not a reason to become disheartened or abandon our journey. It is just a stumble.

Today, I will not be discouraged by mistakes or delays. With each stumble, I will remind myself, "I am on the right path; I am up to the task."

Obstacles are those frightful things you see
when you take your eyes off the goal.

—Hannah More

•

Reality is something you rise above.

—Liza Minnelli

•

If at first you don't succeed, you're probably lucky.

—Margaret L. Clement

I am still learning—how to take joy in all the people I am,
how to use all my selves in the service of what I believe,
how to accept when I fail and rejoice when I succeed.

—Audre Lorde

•

When you get into a tight place and everything
goes against you, till it seems as though you could not
hold on a minute longer, never give up then, for
that is just the place and time that the tide will turn.

—Harriet Beecher Stowe

You may have a fresh start any moment you
choose, for this thing that we call "failure"
is not the falling down, but the staying down.

—Mary Pickford

•

The secret of joy is contained in one word—excellence.
To know how to do something well is to enjoy it.

—Pearl Buck

One woman's journey: Sally Ride, astronaut

When Sally Ride was a student in California, she wavered between two extremely different career paths: scientist or tennis pro. She chose science, embracing the discipline of graduate work in laser physics. Her career seemed destined to be one of research and teaching; then, in 1977, she saw a newspaper ad that would change her life.

NASA was looking for scientists to join America's space program as astronauts. Sally had never even thought of such a path; indeed, few women at that time would have done so. She had already launched a career as an academician. Why make such a dramatic change now? The space program was notoriously demanding. The rigors of space travel—weightlessness, stress, danger—were well known. Would she be accepted? Could she succeed? She had to try. And she succeeded admirably. In 1983, Sally Ride became the first American woman astronaut.

Her dilemma was one that we all face in our lives. Should we follow a path already set out, or a more unusual one, for which we have no guidelines? Should we play it safe or take a risk?

For most of us, our greatest growth will come when we take a risk or forge ahead into a new frontier. Our deepest joy will come when we create a destiny for ourselves that most people never even dream of. All it takes is the courage to act when the moment of inspiration comes.

Today, I will look around me for inspiration and act with courage when the inspiration arrives.

The purpose of life, after all, is to live it, to taste experience to the utmost, to reach out eagerly and without fear for newer and richer experience.

—Eleanor Roosevelt

•

We know not where our dreams will take us, but we can probably see quite clearly where we'll go without them.

—Marilyn Grey

And the trouble is, if you don't risk
anything, you risk even more.

—Erica Jong

•

You may be disappointed if you fail,
but you are doomed if you don't try.

—Beverly Sills

•

Every small, positive change we can make in
ourselves repays us in confidence in the future.

—Alice Walker

Life ought to be a struggle of desire toward
adventures whose nobility will fertilize the soul.

—Rebecca West

·

We must leave our mark on life while we
have it in our power, lest it should close up,
when we leave it, without a trace.

—Isak Dinesen

•

The text of this book
was set in Bembo and Isadora
by Sally McElwain.

•